925 THRIFT

# 925 THRIFT

*The Pocket Guide to Finding Silver*

R. E. GOLD

Charleston, SC
www.PalmettoPublishing.com

*925 Thrift*
Copyright © 2023 by R. E. Gold

All rights reserved
No portion of this book may be reproduced, stored in a retrieval system, or transmitted in any form by any means–electronic, mechanical, photocopy, recording, or other–except for brief quotations in printed reviews, without prior permission of the author.

First Edition

Paperback ISBN: 979-8-8229-0800-0
eBook ISBN: 979-8-8229-0801-7

Disclaimer: The publisher and the author do not make any guarantee or other promise as to any results that may be obtained from using the content of this book. You should never make any investment decision without first consulting with a financial professional and conducting your own research and due diligence. To the maximum extent permitted by law, the publisher and the author disclaim any and all liability in the event any information, commentary, analysis, opinions, advice, and/or recommendations contained in this book prove to be inaccurate, incomplete, or unreliable, or result in any investment or other loss.

# Table of Contents

| | | |
|---|---|---|
| | Introduction | xi |
| 1) | Physical Properties of Silver | 1 |
| 2) | Purity and Markings | 6 |
| 3) | Treasure Hunt | 13 |
| 4) | Game Plan | 20 |
| 5) | Authenticity and Preservation | 27 |
| 6) | Triple Crown | 33 |
| 7) | Nuggets | 39 |
| 8) | R&R | 44 |
| 9) | Terminology | 48 |
| | Acknowledgments | 55 |
| | About the Author | 57 |
| | Bibliography | 59 |
| | Notes | 63 |

*But then finally the masses wake up. They become suddenly aware of the fact that inflation is a deliberate policy and will go on endlessly. A breakdown occurs. The crack-up boom appears. Everybody is anxious to swap his money against "real" goods, no matter whether he need them or not, no matter how much money he has to pay for them. Within a short time, within a few weeks or even days, the things which were used as money are no longer used as a media of exchange. They become scrap paper. Nobody wants to give away anything against them.*

—Ludwig von Mises

# Introduction

*A good hockey player plays where the puck is.
A great hockey player plays where the puck is going to be.*
—Wayne Gretzky

Silver is all around us, unrecognized by many but available for those who know where to look. Finding the physical precious metal at undervalued, bargain prices that are unnoticed by a vast percentage of the masses will award you the high ground before the unquestionable value turns mainstream. Securing physical silver will provide a freedom outside of Big Brother's reach. Silver will be a recession-proof asset while future-proofing your wealth.

Silver is part of the foundation for a sound money system. The value of silver was first recognized as far back as 600 BC, when the first coins were struck by the kingdom of Lydia in Asia Minor.[1] Throughout the past centuries, silver has played a major role—mainly in commerce activities. Today, in

the era of unbacked currencies, silver is beginning to shine bright again.

The dollar, a debt-based money system, is dying, along with the other fiat currencies of the world. Fiat currency is any money that a government declares legal tender that is not backed by a physical commodity such as gold or silver. Fiat money has no real value, as market forces such as supply and demand determine its value.

Rising national debts, trade imbalances, supply chain disruptions, government overreach, corruption, inflation, hyperinflation, deflation, stagflation, and shrinkflation weaken and will eventually destroy the trust in all fiat currencies. The worldwide debt bubble, a ticking time bomb and one of the greatest economic threats, will cause society to crumble once it pops.

Despite where social well-being is headed, this demise will neither end commerce nor mark the death of money. New technologies are already changing the way we earn and use money across our planet. The programmed money system we are moving toward will transform and create a whole new class system. Digging deeper, we find this picture might paint a dystopian endgame, as this mouse-click money would be tracked and weaponized. We can only hope that when the curtain is finally pulled back to expose the fabric of lies that many of the unaccountable elite promote, silver and gold will shine as true wealth outside the system.

Silver, considered the poor man's gold, will be instrumental in obtaining financial freedom. Accumulating the physical asset will work as an insurance policy to preserve and provide the necessities of life. When systems eventually break down and fail, having silver as part of a diversified portfolio will open the doors throughout the recovery period and beyond. Helping you learn where to look for the white, shiny metal, identifying your spoils, and understanding why silver is so precious is *925 Thrift*'s main objective. And so follow the advice of the Great One: lace up your skates, get out on the ice, and skate to where the puck is going to be. Stay observant, consistent, maybe a little compulsive, and you will be able to secure a fortune before the ice melts. Let's go!

# 1) Physical Properties of Silver

*Look deep into nature, and then you will understand everything better.*
—Albert Einstein

Silver is one of the most indispensable and prized elements known to man. The unique properties and qualities of silver make it one of the most valued substances found on Earth. Let's flash back to fifth-grade science class and revisit what we learned: What is silver? Where does it come from? What makes it remarkably rare?

Silver is an element on the periodic table with the chemical symbol Ag. Silver is one of the transition metals, part of the workhorse metals of industry. Silver has an atomic number 47, which means there are forty-seven protons and forty-seven electrons in the atomic structure. Silver's atomic weight is 107.8682 amu, and it has a density of 10.49 grams per centimeter cubed. Silver's melting point is 961.76 degrees Celsius, and its boiling point is 2,162 degrees Celsius. Silver has a face-centered crystal structure, and it is one of the most widely known of the noble, inert metals. The element is a white, lustrous, soft, and very resistant mineral.

Most silver is derived from silver ores. Although it can be found in pure form within the earth's crust, silver ore is rarely found isolated in individual nuggets. Certain minerals that tend to accompany silver are quartz, copper (Cu), lead (Pb), zinc (Zn), gold (Au), and sulfides. Locating these minerals can help unearth and identify the silver ore deposits. Once excavated, the silver-containing ore is crushed into a fine powder to expose individual grains that will be chemically processed, thus producing a commercial-grade fine silver at 99.9 percent purity. Silver is found in multiple countries across the world (Australia, Austria, Bolivia, Canada, Czech Republic, Germany, Mexico, Norway, Peru, Russia, and the United States).

The unprecedented properties of silver add to its expanding usability and attraction. Of all the elements known to man, silver is one of the few to be considered precious and rare. It can also claim a few top distinguished prizes as explained below.

**Properties and Qualities**

Below is a brief rundown of the properties and qualities of silver that have led to its status not only as a precious metal in demand for jewelry and coins but also as a metal with many industry uses.

> **Antibacterial and Antimicrobial:** Silver inhibits the growth of microorganisms, including bacteria, viruses, and fungi. Silver is also a nontoxic metal, adding another benefit toward the vital role it plays in the medical field.
>
> **Catalyst:** Silver has unique catalytic properties that make it very useful in the chemical industry. Silver can convert ethylene into ethylene oxide, allowing several organic compounds to be synthesized.
>
> **Ductility:** Silver is ductile. Silver can be stretched into thin wires many meters long. Gold's ductility is the highest of the metals, followed by silver.
>
> **Electrical and Thermal Conductivity:** Silver is the most efficient conductor of electrical and thermal energy of all the precious metals.
>
> **Malleability:** Silver is an exceptionally malleable metal. Silver will not shatter or crack when beaten into thin sheets.
>
> **Optical Reflectivity:** Silver exhibits the highest reflectivity of any metal.

**Resistant to Corrosion and Oxidation:** Silver will not deteriorate by means of chemical or electrochemical reactions. Silver may be susceptible to oxidation, but it is not the same type of oxidation that other metals experience. Oxidized metal that rusts is permanently damaged, while silver oxidation, often called tarnish, can be polished or cleaned.

The technology and medical fields greatly benefit from silver's unique properties. These substantial qualities have made silver a key ingredient in past and present commercial applications and will continue to do so in the future. Because silver is soft on its own, to support everyday use other metals are added to increase its strength. These added metals, such as copper (Cu) or nickel (Ni), decrease silver's purity compared to fine silver. As we move into uncertain times, lower purity forms of silver, especially 92.5 percent silver, are beginning to be sought after and added to diversified precious metal portfolios. Learning how to spot these valuable silver treasures will play to your advantage.

925 THRIFT

# 2) Purity and Markings

*For those of you in the cheap seats I'd like
you to clap your hands to this one,
the rest of you can just rattle your jewelry!*
—John Lennon

Silver comes in many forms, and the purity determines the overall monetary value. Have you ever wondered what the tiny marks or numbers represent on silver objects or jewelry pieces? Legitimate silver is stamped or hallmarked with defined markings to reference the maker, origin, date, and purity. Understanding how to read silver markings, stamps, and hallmarks is an important skill to assist with identifications and time management. These tiny, stamped marks can take the form of pictures, letters, words, names, or numbers. Locations of these hallmarks appear in various places depending on the type of silver piece. In many instances there is more than one marking to identify.

**Millesimal Fineness (MF)**
The millesimal fineness system is used to measure the silver purity in alloys. The system calculates the value by counting the pure silver (parts per thousand) by the metal's mass in the alloy.

**Silver Bullion / Fine Silver (999):** Highly concentrated silver marked *.999 or .9999*. The most important aspect of silver bullion is its 99.9 percent purity.[2] Bullion is usually intended for bars, coins, or rounds and is too soft to be used industrially in manufacturing. Silver bullion is minted and comes in a variety of weights, brands, and designs. Larger ingots, including ten ounces and one hundred ounces, are most common.

**Britannia Silver (950):** Alloy made of 95 percent silver plus 5 percent alloy metal. It is most often marked *950*. Ninety-five percent silver exceeds the requirement for sterling silver, but it is slightly softer than 925 sterling.

**Sterling Silver (925):** With 92.5 percent pure silver, sterling is mixed mainly with 7.5 percent copper alloy to provide strength. Markings include *925, Sterling, STER, STG, SS*, and *Vermeil*.

The most common 925 items are jewelry, serving pieces, and decorative items. These are the treasures that you will have the best luck in finding during the hunt when building wealth.

**Coin Silver (900):** Alloy made of 90 percent silver mixed with 10 percent alloy metal. Objects are most often marked *900*, *Coin*, *Pure Coin*, *C*, or *Standard*. Coin silver cannot be referenced as sterling.

**Constitutional / Junk Silver:** Ninety percent silver content in US dimes, quarters, half-dollars, and dollar coins minted pre-1965/pre-1964 era.

- Barber dimes: 1892–1916
- Mercury dimes (Winged Liberties): 1916–1945
- Roosevelt dimes: 1946–1964
- Barber quarters: 1892–1916
- Standing Liberty quarters: 1916–1930
- Washington quarters: 1932–1964
- Barber half-dollars: 1892–1915
- Walking Liberty half-dollars: 1916–1947
- Franklin half-dollars: 1948–1963
- Peace dollars: 1921–1935

My first realization that there was something peculiar with US minted coins arose when I was a youngster. I remember sometimes scoring a silver Buffalo nickel or a Mercury dime when receiving change at Joe Behr's, the local neighborhood market. Comparing these pieces of silver to the newer coinage raised a flag for me even as a child. A few years later, when I was peddling newspapers for the *Daily Dispatch*, acquiring a silver quarter or a 1964 JFK half-dollar when collecting my weekly paper route money was always a win. These coins looked, sounded, and felt different than the contemporarily clad coins. I knew at an early age that these treasures were unique and held a greater value above their pseudo equivalents. And so the stacking began …

Other nonsterling silver products fall within a range of 85 percent content down to zero. Be aware of each of the following forms to make the best, educated decisions before investing.

> **European Silver (800):** Commonly known as *continental silver*, which is another nonsterling silver alloy. Marks include *800*, *825*, *830*, and *850*, respectively indicating 80, 82.5, 83, and 85 percent silver content. European silver should be collected as part of a diversified plan.
>
> **Silverplate:** Indicating a thin layer of silver coating another alloy. Markings vary by manufacturer. Silver-plated copper and nickel metals can hold a modest value. If priced at a deep discount and self-storage is not an issue, these items can be stockpiled.
>
> **International Silver:** Marked *IS* and means the item is silver plated.

**Alpaca:** Sometimes referred to as *new silver*.[3] Alpaca is an alloy that contains copper, zinc, nickel, and tin. Items will be marked *Alpaca*. Alpaca has no silver content or scrap value.

**German Silver:** Developed in Germany in the late 1800s as a silver substitute.[4] It is an alloy of copper, zinc, and nickel. Marks include *EPNS* (electroplated nickel silver) or *German Silver*. Contains no silver.

**Nickel Silver:** Contains no silver. Marked as *Nickel silver*.

**Electroplated Markings:** *EPNS*, *EPC*, *EPWM*, *EPBM*, and *EPNS-WMM*. No silver content.

## Locations of Marks, Stamps, and Hallmarks

Markings are inconspicuously etched or engraved and are set in places that do not detract from the silver's aesthetic quality. Finding these markings can sometimes be quite difficult, so learning the key places to look will assist in identification. Stamps are usually located on the back or underside of silver items. The novice will gain experience over time when repeatedly handling different pieces.

Hallmarks on jewelry can be found in the following locations: pendants and large, flat items should have a tiny stamp on the back of the item; for rings and bracelets, the hallmark should be stamped somewhere on the interior surface; necklaces and silver chains usually have a stamp near the clasp.

925 THRIFT

Hallmarks on flatware are always marked as either *Sterling* or *Silverplate*. Spoons will have the hallmark on the back handle, usually near the bowl. Forks will be marked near the shoulders or wider portion. Knives and serving pieces will be stamped on the collar or ferrule that surrounds the handle.

Hallmarks on holloware or larger silver pieces such as bowls, platters, dishes, teapots, candlesticks, vases, and other decorative pieces should have the mark on the bottom of the piece. Personal care items such as mirrors, combs, hairbrushes, and dresser sets will be stamped on the underside or on the handle.

Other common sterling silver hallmarks besides *Sterling* and *925* are the lion passant with one paw raised (England), thistle mark (Scotland), crowned harp (Ireland), three towers (Denmark), or three crowns within a cloverleaf (Sweden).[5]

Marks, stamps, and hallmarks provide the clues and invaluable information about the history, value, age, and silver content. Understanding how to decipher these marks will allow you to truly understand the details of your uncovered treasures.

# 3) Treasure Hunt

*Life is being on the wire. Everything else is just waiting.*
—Karl Wallenda

The most common silver unnoticed or ignored by the public is 925. The wealth that hides in plain sight is currently not on the radar of the populace. At the time I wrote *925 Thrift*, the few who saw the value of the innumerable items made of sterling were steps ahead of the masses. As you begin your quest, the sterling available at discounted prices will be your gratifying prize. Congratulations!

Sterling silver jewelry is abundant in countless places within your surrounding area. Implementing a sound plan, utilizing the proper tools, and following the *925 Thrift* recommendations can be highly enjoyable, advantageous, and profitable. What sterling items are out there? What should you be looking for? Where do you look for these treasures? What tools are used to best capitalize on these opportunities?

First, let's determine what should be at the top of your list to pursue. A fundamental mantra: "925 sterling jewelry is my game." Learn it, live it, love it. These 925 "smalls," when picked, will build your base. Jewelry is usually underpriced and mixed in with inconsequential pieces in many of the places that you will be visiting on a regular basis. Jewelry goes unchecked for 925 markings as many do not see the value it holds. The different types of 925 jewelry will vary. Look for the following pieces to examine when on the hunt.

**Jewelry** examples include the following:

- Amulets
- Anklets
- Armlets
- Bangles
- Belly rings
- Body piercings
- Bracelets
- Cameos
- Charms
- Chokers
- Cuff links
- Ear cuffs
- Earrings
- Hairpins
- Lockets
- Medical alert jewelry
- Necklaces
- Nose rings
- Pet tags
- Pledge pins
- Religious jewelry
- Rings
- Tie clips
- Toe rings
- Watches

Larger silver pieces discovered beyond these jewelry examples will bolster your argent reserves. Keep a keen eye out for these kitchen items made of sterling when searching high and low.

**Kitchenware** include the following:
- Apple corers
- Butter pat plates
- Bowls
- Chopsticks
- Coasters
- Creamer and sugar sets
- Cups
- Drinking straws
- Egg cups
- Flatware/silverware
- Goblets
- Gravy boats
- Ice buckets
- Ice picks
- Martini shakers
- Napkin rings
- Nut picks
- Peelers
- Pitchers
- Plates
- Platters
- Porringers
- Pots
- Salt and pepper shakers

- Serving dishes
- Shot glasses
- Soup tureens
- Tea sets
- Toothpick holders
- Trays
- Utensils
- Wine bottle coasters / trays

Additionally, these common utility items made of sterling can be overlooked by the novice. When searching, make it routine to do a second or third lap around when looking for these treasures.

**Common Utility Items** include the following:
- Bells
- Belt buckles
- Bullets
- Candleholders
- Christmas ornaments
- Doorstops
- Hooks
- Inkwells
- Jewelry boxes
- Letter openers
- Lighters
- Matchbox covers
- Magnifying glasses
- Pen/pencil sets
- Perfume bottles

- Picture frames
- Pokers
- Ring holders
- Scissors
- Shoehorns
- Thimbles
- Utility knives
- Vanity dresser items
- Vases

Old vintage toys made of sterling silver are a great addition to a collector's trove. These items are a prize if found.

**Toys and Trinkets** include the following:
- Baby rattles
- Jacks
- Kazoos
- Music boxes
- Musical instruments
- Noisemakers
- Spinning tops
- Toy soldiers
- Trophies
- Whistles
- Yo-yos

These silvery sterling items are overlooked by the naïve and untrained. Inventories will be greatly underpriced by various sellers. The lustrous, white, shiny metal will jump out in unexpected places and will show itself in plain sight as you gain experience in the field week after week.

**Set in Motion…**

I first started thrifting late in life. I was looking for a kitchen table in a high-end, affluent North Carolina town. Mrs. Malfitano, a second mother to me and a lifelong family friend, took me on an adventure one Saturday morning. This eye-opening day eventually led my curiosity to some smaller items that would lead to higher returns. One of my first profitable finds was a pair of women's Versace sunglasses purchased for $1.99 that I later sold on eBay for $498.00. This lucrative sale made the wheels start turning. What could be uncovered in these stores at a discounted price that would be an asset, increase in value over time, and be something I could hold until needed? Sterling was the answer. At that moment, the journey began. Educating myself on the properties of silver and learning the silver markings, stamps, and hallmarks turned out to be outstandingly beneficial in my pursuit.

My first major silver discovery was a sterling silver oblong serving dish weighing 243 grams (7.84 ounces), originally priced at $4.99, and marked down 50 percent with an amber-colored sticker tag. I was at my number one go-to thrift store one early Saturday morning. As the doors opened I beelined toward the silver section. Rummaging through the layers of shelves, I discovered the sterling prize. The sight of the word *Sterling* etched on the bottom of the tray lit my eyes on fire. I soon realized that my weekend morning's amusement could be an opportunity to build a secret wealth.

My notable sterling wins provided a momentum that elevated my motivation into high gear. The rush to build a perimeter and to begin working a routine engineered around a practical, discreet blueprint was my base to build upon.

On your journey you will discover vintage, antique, collectible sterling items that will add steadily to your fortune as your list of assets grow. Sterling pieces passed by and unrecognized by the novice will be your reward. Over time your collection of silver will have created a fail-safe stockpile to help offset any upcoming currency crisis, intense storm, SHTF event, or unforeseen black swan event. In a world where the deck is stacked against us all, the silver accumulated will assist in providing the freedom toward a sense of peace and *tranquillo*.

## 4) Game Plan

*If you fail to prepare, prepare to fail.*
—Steve Prefontaine

The game plan is your strategic edge when building your silver stack. Having the proper tools in your toolbox, self-educating, and carefully preparing with a list of multifaceted sites to frequent before heading out will provide favorable results. Mastering negotiating and bartering skills will reward your efforts at a quicker pace and help strengthen your collection. Be prepared to adjust your plan as you pinpoint the honey holes within your expanding region.

## Tools and References

The following recommended gear will assist you on your quest. Include and utilize these invaluable tools throughout your hunt to gain the advantage. This will ensure the work put forth is well vetted, time is not wasted, and verification toward authentication is provided.

> **Neodymium Rare Earth Magnet:** Made from an alloy of neodymium, iron, and boron to form a tetragonal crystalline structure. Neodymium magnets are the strongest permanent magnet available commercially. This jewelry test magnet is used to check for magnetism and verify sterling authenticity. Magnetized pieces are not 925 sterling. I consider my rare earth magnet key chain as my number one, essential, go-to tool when treasure hunting.
>
> **Magnifier App on Phone:** A general purpose magnifier to view small lettering, clear text, focus, and enlarge is indispensable. Zoom, freeze, and flashlight added features will best assist when viewing stamps, hallmarks, repairs, condition, and quality. Both Android and iPhone applications are available for free in the App Store.
>
> **Diamond Tester:** A basic diamond detector made of metal uses its heated needle tip to cause heat transference when it is placed on the diamond's surface. The thermal conductivity will provide results to determine if the diamond is real or fake; 925 sterling jewelry will have many

gemstones that will escape the seller's attention. These gems will add extra value to one's sterling reserve. A diamond tester can be used at home or in a private setting.

**Digital Jewelry / Grain Scale:** Small portable scale with a backlit LCD display; units of measurement include grams, ounces, troy ounces, pennyweights, carats, and grains. The digital scale can be used at home or in a private setting.

**Reference Books, Cheat Sheets, Phone Apps, and Websites:** Use to source marks, stamps, hallmarks, history, and additional helpful tips. Study, learn, become an expert.

**Phone App:** Hallmarks - Identify Antique: Over 15,000 specific marks conveniently catalogued into categories to make your research easy. There is a search bar to help recognize the marks that identify any valuable precious metal. There is an in-app purchase required to unlock all sections.

**Website:** Online Encyclopedia of Silver Marks, Hallmarks, and Makers' Marks (https://www.925-1000.com): Free, extensive online encyclopedia of silver marks and makers' marks. Over 12,000 silver marks identified. Useful source to identify silver markings used on vintage and antique sterling and coin silver. Also has a section for silverplate marks. This site is very easy to navigate when researching marks and is regularly updated. Outstanding resource.

Next, it's time to do some homework to locate all possible honey holes where the treasure is hidden. Creating a plan to best navigate your surrounding area should include internet and Google Maps searches. Determine locations, days and times of operations, owner information, specialties offered, daily and weekly promotions, additional sister properties, etc.

**Where to Search:**
- Antique malls
- Antique shops
- Antique shows
- Architectural salvage
- Coin shows
- Consignment shops
- Estate sales
- E-waste recycling facilities
- Family attic, dining room hutch, storage
- Flea markets
- Garage sales
- Grandma's silverware drawer :)
- Local coin shops
- Mom-and-pop dealers
- Pawn shops
- Secondhand stores
- Specialty jewelers
- Tag sales
- Thrift stores
- Trade shows

- Used electronic stores
- Wholesale distributors
- Yard sales

**Favorable Internet Searches:**
Craigslist, eBay, Facebook Marketplace, Depop, Poshmark, thredUP, and Decluttr will be positive sources before the masses catch on.

## Learn the Art of Bartering / Negotiating to Win the Rewarding Deals

In the realm of your search, negotiating the deal could be as important as the object that you want to obtain. When you are on the hunt, negotiating, bartering, and trading will be invaluable means to increase profits. Before entering any kind of negotiation, learn to become a skillful and proficient negotiator by adopting the following tips:

- Identify the type of trading partner and educate yourself on the seller.
- Come prepared, be direct, project confidence, and ask questions.
- Research comparable values for what you are looking to acquire.
- Assign a dollar amount to the object.
- Stay within your bargaining range; do not overextend or overbid.
- Don't be afraid to lowball the item.
- Avoid open-ended arrangements.
- Be prepared to walk away.

## Blueprint Modifications

My strategy to accumulate the most silver was to attack planning in a way that best maximized my efforts. I devised a well-thought-out system based on multiple fronts, locations, times of operation, daily and weekly specials, and my favorite honey holes. Efficiently working through the many stores, shops, and markets expanded my good fortune. The saying "Time is money" held true when I was engineering and executing the charge forward. Eventually widening my area of opportunity played nicely into the recreation of the hunt. As time passed, I expanded my search into neighboring cities. The added opportunities and connections wove a profuse and welcome web for me to manage.

As your recon progresses to many sites and treasure troves, you will be able to streamline your routes and strategize an optimum game plan to execute. Larger cities will offer increased opportunities. Smaller towns may provide overlooked gems. Over time the territory will grow as large as you want to take it. The sky is the limit.

# 5) Authenticity and Preservation

*I have often marveled at the thin line
which separates success from failure.*
—Ernest Shackleton

Verifying the authenticity of your silver purchase and properly storing it are most important when investing in silver. If you fail to verify purity and administer the recommended care, time and money will be lost. Fortunately, confirming the authenticity of silver is generally simple. Authenticity tests range from noninvasive to invasive. Following basic care instructions will preserve your wares and further maintain their value.

**Noninvasive Tests**
Noninvasive tests are widely used with some methods being the most reliable. Visual inspection along with the following noninvasive tests will help you analyze and verify your discoveries.

> **Fisch:** Tool used to verify thickness, diameter, shape, and weight of silver and gold coins to determine if they may be counterfeit.
> **Flex:** Silver will flex and may dent, while silverplate does not yield as easily.

**Heft:** Not conclusive, but once you have handled enough silver, through experience you will have a good idea of what the weight should be.

**Ice Cube:** Silver will melt ice quickly; fake silver will melt the ice slowly. Silver is a heat conductor.

**Neodymium Magnet:** A magnet will not attract to real silver. Magnetized silver items will confirm a higher percentage of nickel, cobalt, or iron.

**Ring:** Silver coins when struck with another metal will produce a certain high-pitched bell ring. This test is not a good indicator for tableware. Fake silver will have a dull and blunt sound.

**Touch:** Both sterling and silverplate will have the same feel. Touch is not a reliable test.

**Ultrasound:** A machine measures silver's composition and consistency. Different metals affect how quickly the sound waves pass through. This method can be very expensive, and testing should be left to a professional.

**Visual:** Markings are the best indicator to determine if the object is silver unless it is fake; then you may need to move toward invasive testing to confirm.

**X-Ray Spectrometer:** An instrument that accurately tests any precious metal. The spectrometer uses beams of light to analyze the composition of the metal, and results are then displayed on a monitor, showing the exact content. Jewelers and precious metal dealers tend to have this device.

## Invasive Testing

Invasive testing will provide verification, but it is not recommended as it requires either scraping or the use of harsh chemicals. Chemicals may be dangerous if directions and precautions are not followed. Harm may come to you, or your silver may be damaged, if care is not taken. Invasive testing should only be done at home or by a professional jeweler. Chemicals are extremely dangerous, and invasive testing should not be performed by children under any circumstances.

> **Acid:** Bright or dark color will confirm fine or sterling silver. The acid turns brown with at least 80 percent silver, green with 50 percent silver, or brown and green with silver-plated items. Any other color of the acid reveals different metal.
>
> **Bleach:** Apply bleach to the object. If it tarnishes quickly, then the silver is real. Fake silver will not tarnish. Bleach may damage and devalue the item.
>
> **Nitric Acid:** Apply a few drops to a small silver filing. A creamy-white color will confirm the silver is pure or sterling. A green color will verify the object is silver plated or fake.

## Preservation and Storage

Maintaining silver's sparkle and brilliance to avoid tarnishing can be accomplished by following these preservation tips and care instructions prior to storage. Silver will tarnish when left unprotected and exposed to air, moisture, dust, or dirt. Polish your silver with hot, soapy water, rinsing and then drying thoroughly with a soft cotton cloth. Do not let your silver air-dry as water left standing will cause spotting. Avoid using a dishwasher when cleaning your silver as it will lead to white buildup and a dull finish. Silver carefully dried and correctly packaged will not tarnish easily when properly stored. Wear lint-free cotton gloves when handling your silver as the oil on your hands can accelerate the tarnishing process. Avoid abrasive polishes as they may damage, scratch, or erode the silver's surface. If a polish is required, use a brand-name product and follow the directions. Do not use an old toothbrush, paper towel, or an abrasive cloth as they may mar or damage the finish. Avoid miracle dips as they will take off the finish and give a greenish-yellow appearance. If your silver is heavily tarnished, it is recommended to utilize a reputable jeweler or silver shop for professional cleaning before storing.

Silver should be wrapped in acid-free tissue paper after the cleaning process. Use the appropriate wrapping and then place each piece inside plastic storage Ziploc or cotton bags to protect against structural damage and oxidation. Special tarnish-reducing bags and jewelry pouches also provide adequate protection. Silver should not be stored inside oak furniture due to the wood's acidic nature. Your silver should avoid contact with rubber, plastic, newspaper, wool, felt, velvet, or anything acidic to limit tarnishing and possible damage.

Reusable silica gel desiccant canisters placed within your storage areas are highly recommended to reduce air and moisture exposure. The temperature at which you store your silver is usually not an issue. While hot or cold temperatures are basically safe, avoid extremes such as fire or condensation from excessive frigid conditions.

**The Number One Rule**
Once your wares are cleaned, packaged, and crated, adopt the number one rule and optimum strategy when storing your silver: the top priority when accumulating large quantities of silver is to store your goods in multiple confidential locations outside your home. Vaulting at private, reputable depositories is a safe, secure, insured, and sound option for stackers. Storage should be fully segregated and allocated. Strategically placing caches within your surrounding area, off property from your living quarters, provides an acceptable comfort level and an unthreatening environment.

Avoid bank safe-deposit boxes or vaults as they are considered a poor alternative due to limited bank hours and lack of laws to protect against loss. Bank runs or a debt implosion could cause banks to close indefinitely with no way to access your silver. Also avoid storing any large amounts of silver or gold in your home. Don't set yourself up as a potential mark for burglary or theft. Utilize *all* necessary precautions to keep safe.

Your silver holdings can be stored in a variety of locations and still be readily available at a moment's notice. Calculating and making your storage masterplan a top priority, while walking through each possible scenario will allow you to always stay a few steps ahead. It is better to be proactive rather than reactive in any SHTF event. Take the time to properly store your metals, stay alert, and follow the number one rule. This is your wake-up call—go to work!

# 6) Triple Crown

*You have to remember that about 70 percent of the horses running don't want to win. Horses are like people. Everybody doesn't have the aggressiveness or ambition to knock himself out to become a success.*
—Eddie Arcaro

In the midsummer humidity of Madison County along Route 20 within the pocketed Central New York farm towns, the state's largest antique show brings two thousand dealers together every year.[6] The vendors take over the lime-green horse pastures and spread their goods across multiple show fields. For me, a native New Yorker, taking an annual trip to uncover the silver treasures at this show has always rendered a productive bounty. The annual collectible expo, combined with a swank estate sale in a nearby secluded upstate town and visits to the local village thrift stores, make this the thoroughbred of events each year. Adding to this fair-like atmosphere and topping off the annual event for me, a weeklong holiday spent enjoying family and revisiting authentic childhood friendships holds as true as the most cherished treasures celebrated.

Over the many years of thrifting, negotiating, hunting, and exploring, I have seen scores of silver items. A few memorable items found at local estate sales and antique shows and purchased at sizable discounts were a Georg Jensen sterling silver grape bowl, a Yamaha Finesse Professional solid sterling silver flute, and my most cherished find, a Queen Anne Williamsburg sterling silver flatware complete set totaling 296 pieces.

Educating yourself on the many aspects of silver will give you a greater understanding of its importance. Silver kept on your radar should be revered, appreciated, and respected for its paramount uses.

**Monetary Value and Utility**

> **Default Proof:** Silver will not fail to meet financial obligations over time. Stacked silver acts as a secure insurance policy.
>
> **Divisible:** Silver is capable of being divided. Coins or bars may be scored in the middle to allow you to break them apart into separate pieces.
>
> **High Density:** Silver is difficult to counterfeit due to its high density. Silver's density is 10.5 grams per cubic centimeter. US silver coins have specific weights as determined by the US Treasury. If a silver coin is a gram heavier or lighter than its intended weight, it is a sign the coin may be fake.
>
> **Interchangeable:** Silver responds to changes in times of geopolitical and economic turmoil. Silver strengthens when dollar debasement fears arise and is recognized as a safe haven along with

gold due to the two metals' interchangeable properties.

**Naturally Limited Supply:** About twenty-six thousand tons of silver are produced from mines around the world each year.[7] The only other major source of silver aside from mine production is recycling, primarily of electronics. The demand for silver is high due to uncertainty and added green industry uses. Demand will continue to weaken the available supply, making the noble metal more precious.

**Portable:** Silver is easily or conveniently transported.

**Private:** Silver can be accumulated and personally stored. Many silver enthusiasts state that if you don't hold it, you don't own it.

**Proven Medium of Exchange:** Silver, since ancient times, has been a reliable source of value. The view of economists from across the world is that in a total financial collapse with no reliable currency available, people would revert to a barter system with silver used as the medium of exchange.

**Unit of Account (Silver Standard):** A measurement for the value that is divisible, fungible, and countable. Based on the market value of goods, services, or other transactions, silver can be used as a standard numerical monetary unit of measure or play a role as a price anchor.

> **Wealth Preservation:** Silver is a store of wealth. Silver as part of a well-diversified portfolio will play a role in preserving your wealth. Stored physical silver acts as your insurance policy through dire times.

Silver has a historic value and is beginning to be recognized as its modern-day uses become fundamental. Above silver's monetary and artistic powers, silver holds its primary uses in the industrial/technology arena, medical field, and with personal everyday items. As we move into the future toward a green revolution, the demand is increasing exponentially.

## Industrial, Medical, and Personal Uses

> **Industry/Technology/Green Uses:** 3D-printing applications, air-conditioning vents, artificial intelligence, automobile switches, batteries, car glass coatings, cellular phones, chemical production, circuit boards, computers, drones, electronics, electroplating, engine bearings, explosives, fuel cells, military applications, mirrors, musical instruments, photography, production of antifreeze, robotics, RFID technologies, silver window applications, smart silver textiles, smart TVs, solar panels, solders, space program applications, stained glass making, superconductors, tinted sunglasses, weather modification, and wood preservation.

**Medical Uses:** Dentistry utilizes silver in amalgam for cavity prevention and restoration; hospitals use silver in surface silver-ion spray, medical surgical implants, nanoparticles, silver pharmaceutical creams, surgical mask protection, various medical equipment, wound dressing applications, and x-rays.

**Personal Use Items:** Silver can be used or found in antibacterial clothing, deodorant, laundry detergent, pool purification, smartphone-usable gloves with silver-laced fingertips, and water purification.

As time advances, our scientists' and engineers' creativity will fuel the changing demands of consumers and industry. Several metals and rare earth elements will play major roles in the growth of civilization, but silver, with its unique and versatile properties, will shine high above. Copper may be the highway to electrification, but silver is the glue. The shiny metal holds a bright future and is essential for the advancement of humanity.

The many qualities of silver make it a "Triple Crown" asset. As a wealth protector, industrial-green element, and your insurance policy in times of despair, silver is a vital part of a well-diversified portfolio. With the FOMO and FUD around us today, strengthening your base with some sterling keeps you a few steps ahead of the "blue-pilled." Small moves … get out there and claim your prize.

R.E. GOLD

# 7) Nuggets

*Every silver lining's got a touch of grey.*
—Jerry Garcia

The time and effort I have spent toward mastering the sport of thrifting, rummaging, bartering, and planning have uncovered proven strategies reflective of profitable and personal results. The following tricks of the trade—when used on a regular basis or in tandem as a multi-pronged attack—will assist in attaining goals that you set.

**Foresight**

- All sterling silver pieces, small or large, old or new, damaged or pristine, are valuable.
- Scrap silver will significantly add to your fortune.
- Polishing an item will often reveal hidden markings and other indications of metal content. Skillfully use your tools when on each treasure hunt.
- Locating honey holes, connecting with people, building local relationships, knowing when the discount deals and promotions are scheduled, being the early bird, knowing what to look for, having the desire to learn, being persistent, showing patience, and working out a well-polished plan will produce remarkable results.
- Visit thrift stores, consignment shops, and yard sales in affluent areas. Be the first at garage and estate sales and ask if they have any old jewelry for sale (sellers are usually unaware of which pieces are 925 and which are not).
- Religious, faith-based thrift shops may receive donated estates. Sterling items slip through the cracks and onto the shelves for your discovery.
- Negotiate a bulk deal and then add the desired piece that catches your eye into the overall deal to make the sale move to your advantage.

- Search eBay and use the filter "Best Offer." Sort by "Lowest Price" or "Ending Soonest." Then send out mass lowball bids and be sure to include a well-thought-out message after reviewing the product description and seller's store information.
- Research the old electronics that hold the most silver/gold. Start an e-waste recycling collection business. Host a metals/electronics recycling event.
- Learn and memorize the silver marks, stamps, and hallmarks. Educate yourself on the most common marks to help with time management.
- Check out the jewelry red-tag sales at T.J. Maxx, Ross, and Marshalls. Discounts of 50, 60, and up to 90 percent will be found.
- Barter and negotiate with your flea market vendors. Work the art of the deal.
- Get the first look at the scrap or broken 925 jewelries at your thrift stores. Don't be afraid to ask if they have scrap to sell.
- Seize the moment. You want to be shopping when silver is off the radar. Buy low, accumulate at a discount, and sell high.
- There is always someone trying to talk you out of what you believe. Believe in yourself.
- Befriending a trustworthy jeweler, knowing a reputable appraiser, or patronizing your

local coin dealer will help you gain higher knowledge and appreciation.

**The Golden Nugget**

The strategies and efforts used to stack silver have an ultimate objective. True wealth preservation is the accumulation of gold. Be ready to turn your buds into nugs and recognize when it's time to trade in a portion of your silver for gold bullion. Apply the gold/silver ratio (GSR) to optimize your good fortune. The GSR is the amount of silver it takes to purchase an ounce of gold. To compute the GSR, take the current price of an ounce of gold and divide it by the price of an ounce of silver. For example, the price of gold is $2,000/ounce, and silver is $20/ounce. So 2,000 divided by 20 is 100, reflecting a 100 to 1 ratio. It would take 100 ounces of silver to purchase an ounce of gold. The ratio is a useful indicator to determine the right and wrong times to buy and sell gold and silver. A narrow ratio, for example 20 to 1, indicates that the relative value of silver is up, while a wide ratio such as 100 to 1 indicates that gold's value is up. Use the ratio to your advantage and be ready to turn your bargains into gold.

On your enduring pursuit for precious metals, be generous, kind, and grateful. Turn the invisible into visible. There are countless treasures left unnoticed and still out there to be found. You never know when you may discover a forgotten masterpiece. Have fun on the hunt as your prosperity grows, and you will get by. We will survive.

# 925 THRIFT

# 8) R&R

*While money cannot buy happiness, it certainly lets you choose your own form of misery.*
—Groucho Marx

Over time I have built a small library of books gathered from thrift shops and college-town secondhand bookstores. These are some of my favorites and most interesting reads that have both inspired and entertained me. Keep searching for the truth: it will set you free.

**Recommended Books:**
- *Atlas Shrugged*, by Ayn Rand
- *Beat the Dealer*, by Edward O. Thorp
- *Gold Wars*, by Ferdinand Lips
- *Human Action*, by Ludwig von Mises
- *Medici Money*, by Tim Parks
- *The Art of War*, by Sun Tzu
- *The Big Short*, by Michael Lewis
- *The Creature from Jekyll Island*, by G. Edward Griffin
- *The House of Morgan*, by Ron Chernow
- *The Mandibles*, by Lionel Shriver
- *The Richest Man in Babylon*, by George S. Clason

- *The Wealth of Nations*, by Adam Smith
- *Three Days at Camp David*, by Jeffrey E. Garten
- *Tower of Basel*, by Adam LeBor
- *When Money Dies*, by Adam Fergusson

Bring your sunblock...

## **Recommended YouTube Influencers:**

- Alaska Prepper
- Arcadia Economics
- Bald Guy Money
- Canadian Prepper
- City Prepping
- Financial Prepper
- George Gammon
- Gregory Mannarino
- Heresy Financial
- I Allegedly
- J Bravo
- jeremiah babe
- Kelsey Olive
- Kitco NEWS
- Liberty and Finance
- maneco64
- Marfoogle TV
- Mark Moss
- Minority Mindset
- Miles Franklin Media
- Palisades Gold Radio
- Peter Schiff
- preppernurse1
- Rafi Farber
- Redacted
- Ron's Basement
- SalivateMetal
- Silver Dragons

- Silver Seeker
- Silver Slayer
- southernprepper1
- Stansberry Research
- The Economic Ninja
- Timcast
- The Rich Dad Channel
- Uneducated Economist
- Wealthion
- Yankee Stacking
- Zang Enterprises with Lynette Zang

# 9) Terminology

*Genius without education is like silver in the mine.*
—Benjamin Franklin

**Ag:** Chemical element silver on the periodic table. Atomic number 47.

**allocated:** Separate, set apart from the main mass group.

**alloy:** A substance composed of two or more metals, or of a metal or metals with a nonmetal, intimately mixed, as by fusion or electrodeposition.

**Alpaca silver:** Gray-colored alloy with 2 percent silver content mixed with copper, zinc, or nickel. Sometimes referenced as *new silver*.

**antibacterial:** Destructive to or inhibiting the growth of bacteria.

**antimicrobial:** Destructive to or inhibiting the growth of microorganisms.

**atomic number:** The number of positive charges or protons in the nucleus of an atom of a given element and therefore also the number of electrons surrounding the nucleus.

**atomic weight:** The average weight per atom in a typical sample of the element, expressed in atomic mass units, or amu.

**Au:** Chemical element gold on the periodic table. Atomic number 79.

**authenticity:** Not false or copied, the quality of being genuine, real.

**barter:** The art of bargaining. To exchange in trade, as one commodity for another.

**Big Brother:** The head of a totalitarian regime that keeps its citizens under close surveillance.

**black swan:** An occurrence or phenomenon that comes as a surprise because it was not predicted or was hard to predict.

**blue-pilled:** A fictional pill that keeps one in a world of illusion, taking the pain away from the realities of life.

**Britannia silver:** A silver alloy of high standard, usually 95.8 percent silver content, not to be confused with Britannia metal.

**bullion:** Silver or gold in the form of bars or ingots.

**cache:** A hiding place (noun), or to conceal (verb).

**catalyst:** A substance that causes or accelerates a chemical reaction without itself being affected.

**coin silver:** Silver having the standard fineness for coinage purposes: 90 percent silver, not considered as sterling.

**conductivity:** A measure of the ability to conduct electric current, equal to the reciprocal of the resistance of the substance.

**constitutional silver:** US currency, 90 percent silver coins minted before 1965, sometimes referred to as *junk silver*.

**continental silver:** Sometimes referenced as *European silver*, nonsterling in 80, 82.5, 83, or 85 percent silver content.

**crack-up boom:** The crash of the credit and monetary system due to continual credit expansion and price increases that cannot be sustained long term. In the face of excessive credit expansion, consumers' inflation expectations accelerate to the point that money becomes worthless and the economic system crashes.

**Cu:** Chemical element copper on the periodic table. Atomic number 29.

**currency:** Something that is used as a medium of exchange; money; circulation as a coin.

**default:** To fail to meet financial obligations or to account properly for money in one's care.

**deflation:** A fall in the general price level or a contraction of credit and available money.

**divisible:** Capable of being evenly divided.

**ductility:** The capacity to undergo a change of physical form without breaking; malleability, flexibility.

**dystopian:** A society characterized by human misery and oppression.

**element:** One of a class of substances that cannot be separated into simpler substances by chemical means.

**European silver:** Sometimes referenced as *continental silver*, nonsterling in 80, 82.5, 83, or 85 percent silver content.

**fiat money:** Paper currency made legal tender by an authoritative decree of a government but not based on or convertible into a coin.

**Fisch:** Tool used to detect counterfeit gold and silver coins. Instrument verifies minimum and maximum thickness and diameter, shape, and weight.

**flatware:** Utensils such as knives, forks, and spoons used at the table for serving and eating food.

**FOMO:** Acronym referring to the fear of missing out.

**FUD:** Acronym referring to fear, uncertainty, and doubt.

**German silver:** An alloy of copper, nickel, and zinc. Silver-colored metal that contains no silver.

**gold/silver ratio (GSR):** A common indicator used worldwide. Current price of an ounce of gold divided by the current price of an ounce of silver. Calculation shows how many multiples gold is trading relative to the price of silver.

**green revolution:** A movement to protect the environment.

**hallmark:** Marking on silver that may indicate purity, age, maker, or origin.

**holloware:** Items of usually metal tableware, such as bowls, pitchers, teapots, and trays that have depth and serve as containers or receptacles.

**honey hole:** A discovered place where something of value is found.

**hyperinflation:** Extreme or excessive inflation.

**industrial:** Of, pertaining to, of the nature, or resulting from a manufacturing business.

**inflation:** An abnormal increase in the volume of money and credit resulting in a substantial and continuing rise in the general price level.

**inert:** Not readily reactive with other elements; forming few or no chemical compounds.

**ingot:** A mass of metal cast in a convenient form for shaping, remelting, or refining.

**interchangeable:** Capable of replacing or changing places with something else: mutual substitution.

**junk silver:** An informal term for a silver coin that is in fair condition and has no numismatic or collectible value above the bullion value of the silver it contains. Sometimes referenced as *constitutional silver*.

**keen eye:** A special ability to recognize a particular thing or quality.

**lowball:** An offering that is far less than the seller's asking price as a means of starting negotiations.

**malleability:** Capable of being shaped, as by hammering or pressing.

**market forces:** In economics, refers to the forces of supply and demand.

**millesimal fineness:** System used to measure the purity of different metal alloys, expressed in parts per thousand.

**money:** Gold, silver, or other metal issued as a medium of exchange and measure of value.

**mouse-click money:** Fiat created digitally by the click of the mouse adding to the inflated supply.

**neodymium:** A rare earth, metallic, trivalent element occurring with cerium and other rare earth metals.

**Ni:** Chemical element nickel on the periodic table. Atomic number 28.

**nickel silver:** Silver-colored metal containing no silver content. Sometimes referenced as *German silver*.

**noble metal:** Metallic chemical element that is generally resistant to corrosion.

**nontoxic:** Not of, relating to, or caused by a toxin or poison; safe.

**novice:** A person who is new to circumstances, work, etc.

**nugget:** Anything of great value, significance, or the like; a lump of something, as of precious metal.

**ore:** A metal-bearing rock or mineral, a native metal, which can be mined at a profit.

**oxidation:** The deposit that forms on the surface of a metal as it oxidizes.

**Pb:** Chemical element lead on the periodic table. Atomic number 82.

**periodic table:** A table illustrating the periodic system, in which the chemical elements, formally arranged in the order of their atomic weights and now according to their atomic numbers, are shown in related groups.

**portable:** Capable of being transported or easily carried.

**rare earth element:** Any of a group of closely related metallic elements, comprising the lanthanides, scandium, and yttrium, which are chemically similar by virtue of having the same number of valence electrons.

**reflectivity:** The quality or capability in casting back light or heat, mirroring, or giving back or showing an image.

**segregated:** Set apart for a particular purpose or recipient; assigned or allotted.

**SHTF:** Referring to an undesirable event: shit hits the fan.

**shrinkflation:** A decrease over time in the quantity or in package size compared to the quantity previously sold at the same price point, resulting in a higher cost per unit for the consumer.

**silverplate:** A coating of silver, especially one electroplated on base metal.

**silver standard:** A monetary system in which the standard economic unit of account is a fixed weight of silver.

**smalls:** Lesser, insignificant items found when picking through secondhand items compared to a notable piece.

**stacker:** A person who collects and stores precious metals.

**stacking:** The act of buying, collecting, or taking direct possession of silver bullion, coins, rounds, or bars.

**stagflation:** An inflationary period accompanied by rising unemployment and lack of growth in consumer demand and business activity.

**sterling silver:** An alloy containing not less than 92.5 percent silver, the remainder usually being copper. Often referenced as *925*.

**struck:** A coin produced from a die or coining press.

**synthesize:** To combine (constituent elements) into a single or unified entity.

**tarnish:** To dull the luster of a metallic surface, especially by oxidation.

*tranquillo*: Tranquility, peace.

**unit of account:** A standard numerical monetary unit of measurement of the market value of goods, services, and other transactions.

**vermeil:** Gilded silver.

**wealth:** A great quantity or store of money, valuable possessions, property, or other riches. Anything that has utility and is capable of being appropriated or exchanged.

**Zn:** Chemical element zinc on the periodic table. Atomic number 30.

# Acknowledgments

I would like to acknowledge my children, Ari and Gianni, who motivate me day after day to keep reaching for the stars. I dedicate this book to my father, Frank Orazio, whose spirit, integrity, and love provided a solid, family foundation. Frank's desire for adventure and his triumphs have been an inspiration to embrace life's challenges with confidence and perseverance.

Special thanks to the many YouTube influencers who have provided guidance and invaluable information over the years. Your precious time, shared knowledge, and generosity to better prepare the enlightened are so gratefully appreciated.

# About the Author

R. E. Gold was born and raised in Upstate New York. He is of Italian descent, was raised by loving parents, and is the youngest son of five children. His college interests provided education in engineering, economics, biology, ecology, nutrition, and the culinary arts. Travel throughout his life has allowed him to experience different cultures and people who have helped him shape a better view of how the world works. Music, nature, lifelong friendships, supportive extended family, and an outlook that each following day grants endless opportunities keep him moving forward.

# Bibliography

Castner, Leon. "Silver Mark Identification." National Appraisal Consultants LLC. April 3, 2019. nacvalue.com/silver-marks/.

Churchill, Alexandra. "What Is Coin Silver Flatware and Is It Worth Anything Today?" Explore Martha Stewart. July 2, 2021. marthastewart.com/8104180/collecting-coin-silver-flatware/.

Claus, Patricia. "The World's First Coins were Minted in Ancient Lydia." Greek Reporter. March 4, 2022. Greekreporter.com/2022/03/04/worlds-first-coins-greek/.

Cochran, Steven. "18 Best Quotes About Silver." Gainesville Coins. Sept. 15, 2022. gainesvillecoins.com/blog/famous-quotes-about-silver/.

Cochran, Steven. "What is Silver Bullion? Everything You Need To Know." Gainesville Coins. Aug. 30, 2021. gainesvillecoins.com/blog/what-is-silver-bullion/.

Coles, Bennett R. "Standard Nonfiction Disclaimer for Copyright Page." Cascadia Author Services. accessed Oct. 12, 2022. cascadiaauthorservices.com/disclaimer-for-copyright/.

"Difference Between Pure Silver, Sterling Silver and Coin Silver." Orion Metal Exchange. Nov. 26, 2019. orionmetalexchange.com/difference-between-pure-silver-sterling-silver-and-coin-silver/.

Fisher, Daniel. "The Physical Properties of Silver." Physical Gold. July 11, 2018. physicalgold.com/insights/the-physical-properties-of-silver/.

"Gold Silver Ratio." GoldSilver. accessed Oct. 24, 2022. goldsilver.com/price-charts/gold-silver-ratio/.

Gray, Theodore. *The Elements: A Visual Exploration of Every Known Atom in the Universe.* New York: Black Dog & Leventhal Publishers, 2009.

"How to Identify Sterling Silver Marks & Numbers?" Noname Antiques. accessed Sept. 19, 2022. nonamehiding.com/sterling-silver-marks-and-numbers/.

"How to Test Silver." Silver Recyclers. accessed Aug. 9, 2022. silverrecyclers.com/blog/how-to-test-silver.aspx.

Kenton, Will. "Barter (or Bartering) Definition, Uses, and Example." Investopedia. Feb. 18, 2022. investopedia.com/terms/b/barter.asp.

Miller-Wilson, Kate. "How to Store Silver Without Tarnishing or Scratching." Love to Know. June 14, 2022. antiques.lovetoknow.com/about-antiques/how-store-silver-without-tarnishing-scratching.

Mises, Ludwig von. *Human Action: A Treatise on Economics*, 428. San Francisco: Fox & Wilkes, 1996.

Negi, Chandan. "75 Best Jerry Garcia Quotes on Love and Life." Internet Pillar. Sept. 3, 2022. internetpillar.com/jerry-garcia-quotes/.

"Silver Identification Guide." Kovels. accessed Sept. 26, 2022. kovels.com/marks-identification-guide/identification-help/silver-identification-guide/.

"Silver Quotes." BrainyQuote. accessed Aug. 27, 2022. brainyquote.com/topics/silver-quotes/.

"Silver Quotes." Goodreads. accessed Aug. 27, 2022. goodreads.com/quotes/tag/silver/.

Treebold, Jim. "How to Check Silver Authenticity." Encyclopedia.com. Feb. 5, 2018. encyclopedia.com/articles/how-to-check-silver-authenticity/.

"Uses of Silver." All Uses Of. Oct. 24, 2021. allusesof.com/metals/uses-of-silver/.

Weatherford, Jack. *The History of Money: From Sandstone to Cyberspace*. New York: Three Rivers Press, 1997.

"What Is Junk Silver?" CoinCollecting.com. March 3, 2022. coincollecting.com/what-is-junk-silver.

# Notes

1. "The World's First Coins were Minted in Ancient Lydia," Greek Reporter, March 4, 2022, greekreporter.com/2022/03/04/worlds-first-coins-greek/.
2. "What is Silver Bullion? Everything You Need To Know," Gainesville Coins, Aug. 30, 2021, gainesvillecoins.com/blog/what-is-silver-bullion.
3. "What are Nickel Silver, German Silver and Alpaca?" the spruceCRAFTS, Oct. 2, 2019, thesprucecrafts.com/nickel-german-silver-alpaca-149118.
4. the spruceCRAFTS, "What are Nickel Silver, German Silver and Alpaca?".
5. "Date Code Marks on Swedish Silver," Online Encyclopedia of Silver Marks, Hallmarks & Makers' Marks, accessed Oct. 12, 2022. 925-1000.com/Fsweden_Date_Code.html.
6. "Madison-Bouckville Antique Week," Madison-Bouckville Promotions, accessed Oct. 24, 2022, madison-bouckville.com.
7. "Is Silver in Short Supply? Silver Demand vs. Supply," GOLDCO, accessed Sept. 19, 2022, goldco.com/is-silver-in-short-supply-silver-demand-vs-supply/.

*Gold is the money of kings,
silver is the money of gentlemen,
barter is the money of peasants,
but debt is the money of slaves.*
—Norm Franz

www.ingramcontent.com/pod-product-compliance
Lightning Source LLC
LaVergne TN
LVHW012034060526
838201LV00061B/4606